Broken but Still Beating: Poetry from the Heart

Michelle Warren

BookLeaf Publishing
India | USA | UK

Presentation by *BookLeaf Publishing*

Web: www.bookleafpub.com

E-mail: info@bookleafpub.com

ISBN: 9789358317190

First edition 2023

*For all the women who have experienced or
felt, in some way, any of what this poetry
explores. I see you!*

ACKNOWLEDGEMENT

Writing this collection of poetry was a raw and cathartic process. This would not have been possible without all those who inspired these poems; whether positively or negatively, they played a part in this experience. I also am extremely grateful and appreciative of my dear friend, Kerry (aka Mo), an incredible editor and writer who lent her editorial expertise to this collection as well as the title. I express my heartfelt gratitude to my parents for always supporting and believing in me, which makes it easier to embark on creative endeavors like writing a book. Lastly, I extend my appreciation to BookLeaf Publishing and the editorial team there for helping me throughout and making my musings a reality.

PREFACE

This book of poetry was written as part of the #TheWriteAngle Poetry Competition (November 2023) through BookLeaf Publishing. Poetry is not a form of writing that I have much experience with, but I'm working on changing that, one word at a time.

Grandma's Hands

An oven mitt
Decades of use
A little tattered, a little worn
The big spoon with
The oversized handle
Made for hands needing
Extra help, more grip
Used only a few years
The gentlest hands
I ever knew
In the kitchen, opening an oven
Protected from the heat
Scooping some jelly for toast
Two things that I hold dear
Many more I also have near
Reminds my heart, shakes my soul
Those hands, always helping
Folded in prayer
Last time I held them
Battered and bruised
Never did they cause pain or harm
They worked with love all around
Wrapping bandages, wiping tears
Clapping for kids doing their thing
Folding the towels
Hands cupping a pup's wrinkled face

Fingers glide over
A little white dog
Patting backs and holding
Pens, words flowing
To family and friends
Rolling noodles with
Delicate care, love
Baked into sliced
dough
Happily holding
A cup of chai tea
Held gently
Including me
Gripping a walker
Places to go
The best hands
Never stay long enough though
Only memories now
Of the sweetest touch

Fairytale Nightmares

Fairytale nightmares
Ebb and flow
there's a high probability
you've been here before,
helping a girlfriend through this sludge,
listening, wiping tears from her face
simply to undo what's been done.
Happily-ever-after comes
With a price
High or low, currency flows
A unicorn, dressed in white
Transformed slowly but
Not really there.
An illusion, sure.
A mirage in the distance offering
the only hydration
to quench her thirst.
Fairytale nightmares
Ebb and flow.

Winter Woes

The sunflower hangs
Weeps for the light
that it's born, trained to seek.
The sun still shines
Yet the warmth is not felt
At all anymore
Darkness comes early now
turns into night where daylight used to bow
Diamond speckles glisten
As summer dew turns its head, frosts
The ground below
Flowers clinging to summer's air
Frozen stiff, iced over without care
Painted skies and painted ground
Red, orange, yellow and more
above and below like a watercolor painting
putting on a show
Fall in Indiana, breathtaking
at times
Other times, winter hurdles autumn and leaves it
behind
No bonfires or trick or treat
Because the air is way too cold
Faces hurt when exposed
Bones ache, joints swell
Those who feel it

Can always tell
When the earth shifts
And pressure builds
Pain radiates through
Straight to Hell
But it's warm there at least
Or so I'm told
Winter's here, here we go
Lucifer's flames dance
Inviting, warm and well
Do I stay or do I go?
Either way I take a chance
Freeze to death
or Burn my flesh

Prey

I learned how to carry
Car keys as a weapon
Before I had a car.
Don't run at night
And never alone
Cross the street quickly when you hear
Their moans.
They'll whistle and holler
Like they are the shit
Mediocre white men
All use the same bit.
They sneer and they bark
Always bullshit
Once it gets dark.
The audacity
Is all they possess.
Cockiness and arrogance
Drip from their brows
I have mace in my purse
My route has to change
To make sure the guy at the light
Won't find me at home.
How ridiculous it is to live this way.
Not all men are mean and want to cause harm
But some of them are
Near and far

Herself

A restless soul
Pretends to sleep
But in the wind
Uneasiness settles
Into the deep ache
That's breathed in
and then
Out
It's been years
Since she's felt like herself
Or maybe that wasn't her
Before all the chaos
Crushed her spirit, energy
Lacking to fuel the fire
That once roared inside
The cold wind howled
That night
As it blew out the flame
Not a flicker
Remains

Me, Too

Looks in all directions
Wagging tongues
Inappropriate
Her age vulnerability sprung
From the creases and corners
Of young and old
First she remembers
A high school hall
Cheerleaders always dressed
For a ball
Short skirts, Pom-Pom smiles
An older boy in the hall
His hands on her quick and fast
Up against the lockers
He's so tall no escape
Then a favorite teacher
Pulls him off
College years, in the aisles
Grocery shopping now
Dials danger in, they're following
Her past the cereal
Out the door
her feet move swiftly
They're distracted by the mess she left
she's safe
But just for now

A wrestler date he brags to her
About an assault he led
She's trapped again
but she's not his type
This time it's what
He said
Next time
A different boy, it's getting late
Strong and rough
Forearm force held her down
A wrestling move he knows well
Pin and hold from his left side
A hand slaps down
Across her mouth
Rage flashes in her eyes
But only for a moment
He won't get satisfaction
Or a moment of pride
The whisper echoes in her mind
"Go ahead and scream,
No one will hear"
She's out now, and wonders
How did this happen
But on to the next, fresh
Out of college
A musty newsroom
Old and tired with a new
Dress code, be sure
To know she likes pants

The big boss though
Gross and rude reminders daily
Short skirts only for her
All alone, a man in power
She doesn't cower and doesn't move
even the next time
Another "boss" sends her out
"Put on a dress, a high hemline"
This client won't buy
if you aren't a good time
She never spoke, not a word
Of the mediocre men
Who stalk her dreams still
After all these years
Time goes on and there's
More, don't shed tears
Don't let them win
Grown up now she has her voice
Down the hall, a bathroom break
A group of them working
A casual encounter turns to
Sneers, "a party in his pants"
Is what she hears
Disbelief, yet again
They're professionals: this is absurd
It's time to talk, file a report
Handled badly all in a room
They block her in
Wedged against the windows

that don't open no
Escape the room is small
Caving in
Lungs are squeezed, muscles twitch
is this a nightmare
Is she awake?
They lie and fumble their well-planned excuse
"Paint on my pants" is their new-found verse
It's too much, eyes swell
she's too tired to fight their lies
Salt water melancholy
from all the years
Bundled up anger drips
In her tears
5 against 1 and there's no proof
even an eye witness isn't enough
Nothing happens back to work
All in the same building
Pass in the halls
In a haze she now knows why
She was quiet for so long
Even when it's obvious
The men have it all
The power and the rights
This is why so many
Don't try
Hush their truths
It's quiet now
Just below the surface though

Rage always roars
And we all will one day
Break old rules
and scream together
"Me, Too"
At those damn men
Those Fools

Out of Touch

I'm no longer in touch with her
Or her or her either
She broke my trust
More than once
She made poor choices
Rained chaos on my life
She settled for less
Than she deserved
Never trying hard enough
To make a change
Comfortable unhappiness
Knowing what to expect
Made sense, felt better
Than rocking the boat
The unknown terrifies
Nothing's the same
What would happen if she did
Push back, force a change?
I'm no longer in touch with her though
So who's to know?
All those old versions of me

Heartbreaking Sounds

Is this what it sounds like
When a heart breaks?
Silence, silence
Except breath, no words
No conversation
Slamming doors
Words that cut
I know how the saying goes
But words really can hurt
Draw blood from the jugular
Gurgling, choking
Breaking a heart can be quiet or loud
No auditory acknowledgment
Or decimals of noise so loud glass shatters, dogs
howl
Splinters gorge into a slow-beating heart turned
to stone
Some fights are not
Fair in this game
Of life
Some choose not to play nice
No sharing, only hoarding
All the toys
Is this what it sounds like
When a heart breaks?
I hear colors

See thoughts
Feel words or lack thereof
The clock ticks toward the end
Can a heart split in two
Still keep a beat?
Is pumping blood required
For both sides
Pain radiates through the bones
Skips the chest and hits a knee
Stumbling, wobbling down
She goes
Nerves scream fire burns
The heart feels nothing
Barely there
Searching for a reason
To try and heal
Nothing's there, never was
Only a mirage a scarred heart
Drew the lines zig-zag
To and fro on
A monitor, low beeps
is this what it sounds like
When a heart breaks?
Surrounded by people
But always alone
A smile missed
There should've been more
Grasping at straws
Clutching air

Deep in her chest
Hollowness stares
Back in the mirror
Before the rise
Nothing new another day
Passes
What's the point?
Who's to say?
Sadness wrapped around
like a heavy shawl
White-knuckle grip
Won't let go
Afraid to live, try and move on
She's not sure what that takes
Is this what it sounds like
When a heart breaks?

My Bro

Nothing but love in a heart of gold
Others try and be him but they fall short
Always helping those in need
However he can, there's no doubt
When there's a call to make he ensures it's fair
All around sarcasm flows
You might not know what he means
Nevertheless there's a guaranteed laugh
Every day he does more, to help this world open
doors

Hidden Scars

Invisible pain
Bones heal and bruises fade
A left hook with sharp words is harder to treat
There's no cast or ice pack
To numb the pain
Just because they can't see them
doesn't mean they aren't there
Hidden Scars
Nobody stares at those emotionally abused
They can't see through the filter
They choose
Cast a glance
Over there
She looks like someone
Who might understand
Timid demeanor
Soft-spoken tone
I probably know
What happens when
She's not home alone

The Fall

Guarded heart
After the descent
Broke in pieces
Razor sharp, never dull
Indifference sets in
Evidently there's too much
Love like that never dies
Always ablaze under the ash
Damned if you do damned if you don't
A lot has changed but not all of it
Memories flash of years gone by
She won't be able to survive
Another fall

Work, work, work

A nervous shake
Underneath the skin
Inside the body, soul
Head is spinning
Anger sprouts
Drown it out quickly
Before anyone shouts
Work and work and work
Some more
There's still not enough
Money for
Needed things and
Wants this job
Takes the joy
Right out of my heart
Beating faster, nerves are shot
She'd make a change
But where to start
Comfort keeps her
Miserable
Knowing what to expect
Somehow stops her
Leaving the grind
She'd take a step
Leave it all behind
Would it bring peace

Or a different kind of
The same uneasiness?
Nobody knows
Especially her
She's paralyzed
Frozen, stuck
Until she finally goes

POV

How are you
Not sick of me yet?
A tornado torn through
your life
More times than not
A Gypsy spirit pulls me
All around and my beating
Heart ricochets back
Every time
Magnets pulling
Toward one another
You think it's only the idea
Of you that torments me
Wants more of you
Than you're willing to give
I can see your point of view
and maybe
If I were you
I'd see it that way, too.

Saturday Night

I'm a little tipsy
Clawing for your attention
You dismiss me
Your morals are high
You're a good guy
I've been drinking
So your office
Is off limits
One of many reasons I'm so
Drawn to you
My makeup is smudged
And I want you to see
Me in this state of
Vulnerability
You've seen it before
Many times
If I behaved like this more
Maybe I wouldn't have
Missed the best love of
Them all, always true
In my mind and heart
They're calling for you
Would you ignore me?
Would you call my name?
If I came looking for you
Would you feel the same?
I'm all over the place

Here and there
I reach for you
But only air
Imagination takes hold
I picture us
Once again
Bodies tangled
On the floor
Move over now toward
the door you're far away
Touch and sparks
Desire builds
Wanting, needing
On your mark
Get set
Once again back
In time
Love was pure, innocent, new
Carried with me and maybe you
All these years to and fro
Others came and others went
None held on
To like each other
It's late the day is gone
Tomorrow's here where to go
It won't be long though
Nothing new
Knock knock
I'll be coming for you

Jitters

Excitement
Builds, overflows
It's been a long time
Since I've felt this way
This me is smiling
Almost a giggle
Of anticipation
A football game
I do want to see
But a useable excuse
Is fine with me
Shower, shave
All the right things
A jersey, a sweatshirt
I'm fangirling today
Rain, dark clouds
There's a chill
On the air yet
There's warmth in
His touch and cold
Nowhere to be found
She's been freezing,
wasting away
silently crumbling, untold
Now she feels sunshine
Warmth on her face

She begins to thaw
Awakened at last
Back to his arms
Her most favorite place
present and past

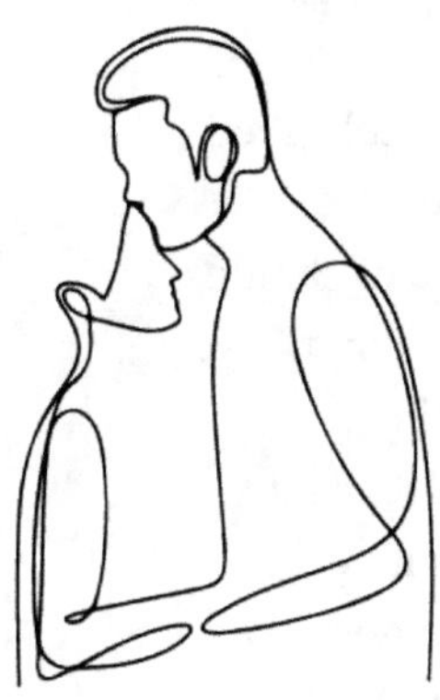

Debt

A smirk
She thinks to herself
How this is not like her
Or maybe it is?
She bites her lip
Wonders what if
About so many things
In love and life and loss
A selfish move feels good
Herself put first
Such a rare type of should
Heat and flesh, hungry eyes
And hands, feeling,
Searching for deep sighs
And then a moan heat
Travels fast when you're
All alone should I ask
Or just surprise
Wonder what he'd do
If I arise from my slumber
In his bed
She was thinking about
Him again his blue eyes
Staring into her soul
Talk is easy never cheap
All the things in her mind

Trusting him
Secrets and dreams
safe now his to keep
He was the first and always the best
Her body remembers
Every encounter rest
Assured she always
Will be thankful
And indebted to him
What he taught her
She learned well
An eager student
Craving more
In the morning hours
As the sunrise shows
Her beating heart
Still knows
What it beats for

Warm Winters

Wind-chilled air
Cuts to the bone
Summer's gone
Fall is fleeting
Winter comes knocking at the
Door but uninvited pushes through
The rain nips your nose
Frosted feet and frozen toes
Roar the fire roasting logs
Call the heat into the home
It's gross outside but nice in here
Grab a blanket
Comfy and warm
Snuggle up next to him
What a beautiful sight
On this otherwise cold, dark night

Unequal

Whore
Slut
Bitch
And
Ho
These are the things
They call, you know
Never the boys oh not them
The girls get shamed
While the boys high five
And pass the blame
Onto the next one
Not staring in the mirror
Reflections they see
Don't bring tears there's
No crime
If the Y chromosome
Pops in time
"A man's world"
I hear them say
Sit down ladies
There's no equal pay
Maybe tomorrow
But not today

Insomnia

It's already tomorrow
Twice in a row
The days ran over
While I'm still awake
No sleep
Yesterday was incredible
Amazing and fun
Never been so reckless
So wild or free
Finally put the focus on me
Football Sundays have always
Been great even as a kid
I'd stay up late
Watching and rooting for the good ol' Bears
I love Sundays they're my favorite again
I took back some power
Hard and fast
It felt so good
to have
Some control at last
Give and take
Don't ever ask for what you won't reciprocate
Body and mind deserve a break
Yesterday's escapades
For goodness sake
Blessed multiple times

Shake and bake
Muscles are sore
Haven't been worked
That hard hardly at all
Daydreams linger
Longer than they should
Distractions like these
Are never good
When the time clock
Is ticking, there's work
To be done
Back to the grind
At least for now
Figure out how
To replay the day
Two old friends
Learning their way
Around again
Navigating curves
Once known by
Heart
Find a new route
One more time so
Maybe now they can
stay and play

Hunger

Leftover Thai food
A bottle of wine
Pair nicely with
Her deep sigh
She's still hungry
Thirsty, too
Never satisfied
Never full
Wipe her mouth
She's drooling now
A deep ache
way down inside
Flashbacks
Crack back and forth
She feels the pull
Known all too well
She wants him
And he's not there
Years of longing
Wishing, waiting
To repair a break
Done by her hands
Glue it back together
Tape it up
Make it strong enough
This time to hold up

Not bend or fracture
Handle with care
Broken can be beautiful
So make it pretty
We can't have a dream
Become a nightmare
Remove all barriers
Every one that's there
No more hurdles
No more pain
Happily-ever-after
Might really be true
It's up to her to do
What must be done
She's off now
Like a runaway
Train
Crash and burn
Or stay on course
We'll find out
At the turn.

Imaginary Son

He would have been
Kind-hearted, a sweet
blue-eyed boy, I'm sure
Whom we would love
And teach new things
How to use a spoon
Ride a bike, wear a
Baseball glove
He would have been
"Unplanned"
Unexpected, too
Regardless of the timing
He would have been me and you
What we would have called him
There are some thoughts on that
It's weird to think about now
Thirty plus years after the fact
"Logan" is a good choice
Strong and brave and true
Plus a little nod
to Marvel Comics, too
Maybe he was born
Midnight December 7
Right where he should be
In between you and me
We would have loved him as a baby and beyond

Just kids ourselves
But we knew more than some
Liked to think about
He would have created
Chatter, disapproving glances
I'm sure
Nonetheless he would have
Ignited a wildfire of joy as well
Who wouldn't love a baby
Adored by his mom and dad
We would've done so many things
Taught him wrong and right
Shared our stories of our struggles
Examples he could store
For one day when he grew up
He might need to use them more
He is a dream of mine I visit
Time to time
Never created in this realm
But on the other side
Where possibilities flowed
Like water
Hard times were never there
If he had been a possibility
Oh what my heart would see
His younger siblings
Old enough to be his kids now
The fun I'm sure they'd have
Sadly he was never here

Not able to be seen
Only imagined in my mind
When memories rewind
To watch him grow and live and learn and love
him through it all
He would have been the greatest gift
A way to give some more
His dad would have stayed with me
And we would've done our best
Crazy as it seems
I think we would have passed the test

Speechless

Numb to the touch
Inside and out
Feelings once held
My heart
Connected my spirit
Long gone now
There one minute
Not the next
Open my mouth
Nothing comes out
Words caught in my throat
I can't speak
But I have no doubt
There are unhappy people
Bound together only
In time
Deserve more than
What they're getting
Giving nothing
Play the parts
Things look good
Outside their hearts
Typed responses
Only for show
This way nobody
Will ever know

What's real and true
Everyone looks better
On a screen
Nothing new
To get into here
Save face
It's only time
Wasting away
Day by day
Tick tock
Goes the clock
Every minute
One by one
Adds to the total
Already gone
Hours, days, months, years
Without action
Without a voice
Speak up, child
It's your life
Being alive
Doesn't mean
Living, take it
Back, you're in
Control
The silence so loud
It hurts my ears, aches in my head
Your story deserves
More pages – blank, shiny and new

Fill them with dreams and fun
This time, let yourself run
Don't let this chapter
End the book
There's more to do
Before it ends
Read it slowly line by line
Regret is a heavy load
To carry, wears you down
Breaks your bones
Pressure builds
You're already alone

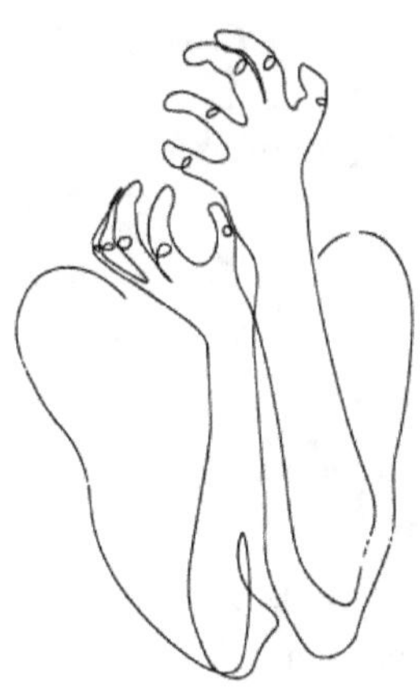

Existence

She feeds it daily
Yet it starves her soul
His existence
Can't be ignored
So long ago, innocence
Peaked does it make sense
To doubt all the rest?
Compare them all
To love once known
Nobody comes
Close to the feelings
He stirs up again
And again
A beautiful friend
Who has earned the most
Trust, he's
All that she wants
Her trust in him
May not be returned
Past mistakes haunt her
Dreams and days
Bad choices, decisions
That broke more than
Bones

Your Turn

It's good to feel
Wanted
To want to be
Seen
To see the best
In someone who's
Better than the rest
For you there's nothing
Selfish
When someone finally notices
Wants you with
Obvious effort
It's a beautiful thing
Rare and mysterious
Many seek but never
Find this coveted treasure
Like a fairy in the garden
You someday hope to catch
Pay attention listen well
There is someone out there
Looking
Waiting
Wanting
to see you
Love you, adore you
And more

They are real and they are there
Just be patient, my dear
Your turn is coming, too
Soon you'll feel
The change
As tables turn
The heat from a touch
Hot enough to burn

Heavy Blanket

I'm so tired
Every day
Sleep enough
It doesn't matter
Two hours or 10
It's all the same
Fatigue takes hold
Body and mind
Weighted down
Slow to move
Slow to think
Decision-making
I don't recommend
This heavy blanket
Pulls me down
Makes it hard to
Even breathe
I'll take a nap
But never notice
Repeat the steps
Day after day

Time to Fight

Some days I still feel
The weight, heaviness of
What's going on
In this broken-hearted world
And in my head
Hectic drama every once in awhile
Stressful panic rises quickly
What is best, what should I do?
They have issues, I feel stuck.
My problems overflow, pile all up
It's all too much
This and that
Moving fast
Try to breathe
Can't catch my breath
Settle down this won't last
Tell myself look at the past
Every bad day in the rearview mirror
Even though some made me
Want to bow out
Forever, permanently leave
It all behind
Maybe at my funeral they'd see
How unkind
They'd been, stress they caused
Who knows though?

Some just are what they are
I feel better in the sun
Winter's coming, I come undone
But think again of all the good
Family, friends, pets and more understood
Stress is a given but giving up is a choice
Stay and fight to make things right
Help your kids navigate life
There's so much here
To battle the pain
Even on the rain-filled days
Look inside or to a friend
You know you can find
A way to mend
The cracks you feel all over you
Fill them in however you can
It's time to fight
Take a stand
The world needs you
Hug yourself tight
Be ready for the next
Cold, dark night

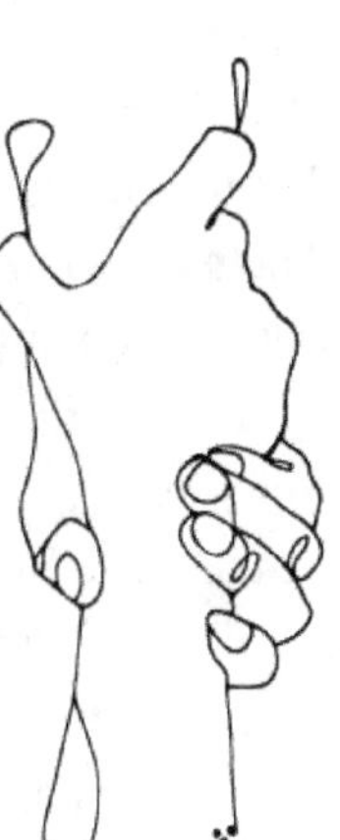

Lonely Girl

Sadness sneaks
In quietly
So as not to disrupt
Be noticed
Initially
Then knocking
Softly on your
Mind's heartbeat
Thump thump
The pain bounces
Temple to temple
Tears are tiring
Salty, too
Streaks and burns
Rewind the tape
Make it new
There's a chance
It might skip you
Lonely girl
You'll be okay
Just remember
What to say
Speak your truth
All of it
Tomorrow is a new day.

Night Moves

If I was there
Or you were here
Sleep would no longer
be what I longed for most
you see
Tired eyes would open wide
A burst of energy
A wild ride
Dreams and rest
They can wait
I'd like to show you
How I shake
Guide your hands
To my back
Pull me close
Breathe me in
Hands on me hands on you
I know you know what to do
Touch my face
Soft and slow
Hands explore
Please don't stop, I want more
I need you now
Touch me please
Everywhere you can reach
Your mouth moves quickly

To my neck
Tip my chin
Heads spin looking back
Dizzy dancing
Moves to make
Whisper to me
What you crave
A willingness in my soul
Shivers run
down my spine
Fingers now intertwine
Lay me down
Next to you
My favorite place
Is just right here
Anywhere you are near
Touch me tease me
Make me moan
Sleep will come
Once we're done

Shrine

I'm so tired
Even though I sleep
My body collapses inside of me
I think I'd cry
But the energy's gone
Weighted blankets hang
From my bones
Or maybe heavy, wet towels
Pulling me toward the ground
It's a battle to hold my head up
Straight pain radiates down
My spine and twists my shoulder
Socket left then right
Electric shock shivers
Down my arm
Hand goes numb
Sound the alarm
Eyes wide open
Then they're shut
Slow blinking, hard
To hold open
The pain's too much
Shoulder socket catches
Clutches the ache
Moves to my chest
My heart might break

Living like this takes a lot
Out of me
I wish others
Could see
Invisible pain
Torments me
Day after day
It's all the same
A shrine to pain
That's my legacy

Here and Now

God I miss you
Like I'm 16
It's been a day
and that's too long
I long for your touch
Please wait for me
There's no key
To turn back time
But maybe now we will see
What's directly in front
Of you and me
No more looking left and right
Cross the street, in plain sight
Grab my hand, wrap me up
Let all the sorrow, regret and pain
Walk with us a little while
Around the turn
Take a bow
Let it go, it's on its way
Joy and love are in their place
No room here for broken hearts
They're all mended, here they're whole
Cracks are beautiful anyway
Look closely
all the way through
Notice things missed before

Zoom in to see more
Curl up next to me
The view is nice
Just wait
You'll see

Wandering Mind

Imagination
Creativity sparks
Picture us
In the dark
I know what I'd do
If the pictures in my head
Happened to come true
In the daylight
I know what I'd say
Pull you close
This isn't new
We both know
What the other
Wants to do
Hold my head
Fingers tangled
In my hair
Squeeze your thigh
Breathe in then out
And a deep sigh
One of pleasure never pain
A gentle touch is all it takes
Snuggled up close
Movie time
Make the most
Of the minutes

As the clock strikes
In the depths of hearts and souls
Way down deep near pelvic bones
There is an ache a pulse that takes
Over thought and reason
You feel so good
Next to me
My mind wanders back
To days before
When this feeling was in
The palm of my hand
Held and carried
Protected
If only just in my head

Reflection

All the years
I realize I have lived
Only snippets and moments in
Time reflect like a camera flash
In the mirror
Where I look at the face
That looks like mine
Who was I?
Before this day
When all the years
Added up
Mistakes knocked down
Like Dominoes
back then
The old me,
She's different than
The reflection
In the mirror
In this moment
On this day
I am the only
Me left to make it
All okay
Things I've done
Things I've said
Some cut my flesh

Some open old wounds
Some things better left
Buried where they are
Birthday candles
All ablaze
So many more than I'd like
To say
Make a wish
Shut my eyes
If only I could go back
One more time

Present Tense

Can't rewrite the past
Nor visit the future
It's all here in the now
What we have and what we lost
Gathered up in my arms
Somehow
Happy tears and rage
Mix together in this particular
Stage
Of life
Present tense
Is all that's left
Love in the moment
Live in the seconds
Passing by one by one
There's still time to
Find your groove
Discover what's buried
in your soul
Learn new things
Don't wait too long
Because it will all pass
We all know
Time doesn't last

Broken Chains

Chains shackled
Around my life
Hold me down
Pull me back
Stop me from
Living
For so long
Break the chains
Find the key
Maybe unlocking them
Is all that needs done
No drama only peace
It's time to start living
Once again
Remember the good times
There were some
Find them and keep them
Tucked away tight
In a pocket or the night light
It's time to take the first step
Going forward
Don't look back
Straight ahead
All you see
So many opportunities

To be your true self
Not wearing a cloak
Trying to fit in
Recognize the fight in you
Once you see it
They will, too

Extra Salt

I taste the tears
They salt the rim
of a margarita glass
Extra salt, just how I like
Drunk on your touch
But the hangover comes
Once you're gone
Refill the glass
Why stop now?
It's over, hung
Up on a myth
Of love lasting
Flames flicker
In those eyes
Reflecting pain
From all the years
Young then old
Look how time flies
When reality is blurred
Nobody hears
These silent cries
In the night, under the covers
Blankets and darkness
Shield the sounds
Of an old lady
Lost

Who is she?
Look in the mirror
What do you see?
She's sad and tired
And she looks
Like me

Breathless

Wrap me up
In your arms
Place your hands
Ones I loved
On my heart
Skipping beats
Inhale exhale
Try and repeat
Out of breath
What comes next?
Pull me close
Muscles tense
I want you and you want me
Messy hair in the wind
Daydreams busted
Melted down
Your lips on me
Feels like home
Eyes wide open
Look and see
Picture perfect
For a moment
Feel something
I've forgotten
What it's like
To be seen
like this

In this Maze

Lonely creeps in
Drips out the corners
Of my eyes
Exhaustion grabs
My head, squeezes tight
I wish I was
Somewhere else
Wrapped in a hug
Or maybe a blanket
In a space soft and warm
Not tonight
And not tomorrow
At least 5 days
Trapped in this maze
Never feeling
Quite whole
Emptiness settles
Deep inside
It's not fair to want
What isn't there
Make excuses
Hope for more
Hope breaks spirits
Though, cracks
To the core
It's hard to breathe

Panic rises
Where to go
There are no options
I'm stuck in this spot
Tears stream now
Inside not out
Hide the truth
Cover the shame
Nobody knows
Who's to blame
Choices matter don't be fooled
Years from now
This could be you

Walk with You Again

If I could walk
With you again
One more time
End to end
Of the old railroad
Tracks we used to hike
Walking stick by your side
I was little back then
That time is gone
Along with you
I miss you more
Every day
If I could walk
With you again
We'd talk about
All kinds of things
Family gone, now at your side
In the fog of my dreams
I step through
into the other side
There's no pain
Only joy
Love spills over
Grab it up
Try and take some
Back across

You and me
Together again
One last time
I'd hold your hand
Fresh and new
And I'd whisper
"Thank you."

The Key

Sitting on your couch
My head tilted to the right
Barely on your shoulder
But enough to feel safe
Even though you never
Should have let me in again
When I came knocking
Softly then harder
On your heart's door
It's been scratched
And forced wide open
The lock is warped
Some fought to get in
I held a key that others had, too
Tarnished from years of being
Gripped in my hand
Long ago I held the first one
Shiny and new
Slipped slowly into the lock,
Somewhat effortlessly
Cracked it open, peaked inside
Raw and starving for what I had
To carry across, to bring in
Excitement, nervousness, first love
Dragged into the open space
A first-time moment
Felt so right

Gave you everything I had,
You gave back willingly
Others came knocking, uninvited
Ended up inside, a place
Much too small for all of us
I made a choice, walked back out
The first door of love I'd known
They swarmed you
And I cried myself to sleep
Key in hand, held close to my heart as it
splintered
For the first time, but not the last
Now as we sit on your couch
Staring at the repaired door
Scratch marks remain there
The key still gripped tightly
In my left hand
And my right,
Showing signs of age
Reaches for you through the years
It was us before any of them
I have the last and only key
I hope he doesn't change the lock
On me

On a Ride with Grief

The rhythm of the horse slow and steady,
Reminiscent of being rocked to sleep
on her G'ma's lap
long ago.
Swaying with the rhythm
of the horse she is once again free.
Peace and comfort coveted.
The funeral loops in her mind.
Winding quietly along the river
the tears continue in this moment,
comfort comes in step
with a horse's gait
and saltwater streaks
on her face a gentle breeze.
wraps her up,
layered on top
of her blanket of grief
she clings to, knuckles
white, she won't let go
not even for a moment.

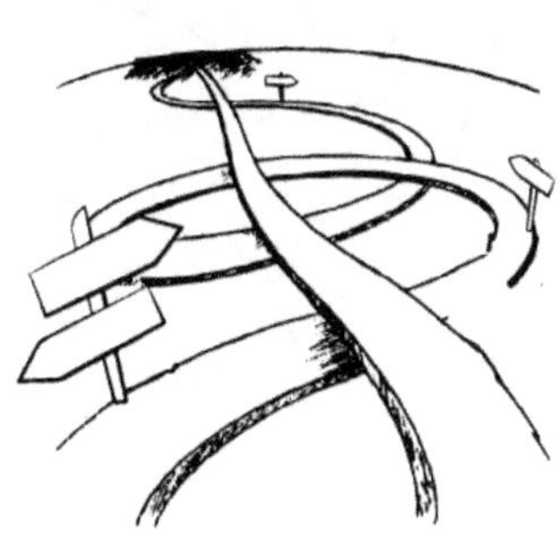

Baggage

A heavy heart
A heavy soul
So tough to carry
Put it all down
Take the baggage
Off of yourself
Unload the pain, grief and despair
It's over now, all a blur
Mark the calendar
Today is the day
For a fresh start
Be on your way

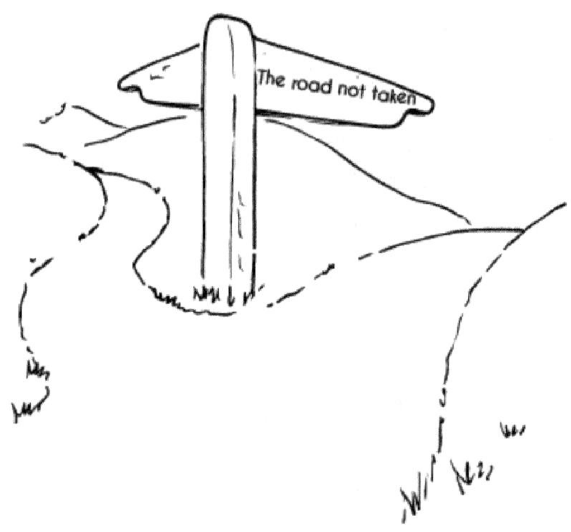

Broken but Still Beating

This heart of mine
Broken but still beating
Feels like my body
And my soul created
Pieces splintered
Here and there
Shrapnel fell
Over there
Darkness now
Where to go
What's real?
It's hard to see
True and false
Only the shadows know
How to breathe the life
Back into me
But they know
And that's what matters
As long as the broken
Still keeps a beat
The rhythm puts
Possibilities within reach
There is hope
To heal this pain
Listen closely
It's up to you

Turn the tempo
Into your favorite song
It's time to dance
In the rain